Praises for

"Marketing Your Church for Growth"

"The sacred and the secular have found a unique meeting point in *Marketing Your Church for Growth*" by Pastor Gary Hawkins. Having been with him on his church campus, I continue to be amazed as to how godly entrepreneurship, wise stewardship and obedience to His vision meet people at their point of need holistically. In this book, you will notice Pastor Hawkins' eye for detail and opportunities that he perceives. But more importantly, his faith and obedience that allow him to take godly risks. All of that is under girded by strong data and honest evaluation. This very practical book will give you simple, inexpensive, godly and pragmatic ways to market your church for growth."

Dr. Samuel R. Chand, President,
Beulah Heights Bible College, Atlanta, Georgia

"Pastor Hawkins has ably demonstrated how we can penetrate society with modern means for Spiritual purposes. Having followed the growth of Voices of Faith firsthand, I am in awe of God's ways and His wisdom which cries out from the streets."

Dr. James Flanagan, President,
Luther Rice Seminary, Lithonia, Georgia

"This book is a must read for anyone who seeks to be a Kingdom Builder in the 21st century. Pastor Hawkins has presented what some would consider a controversial topic in such a simple and powerful way that one cannot deny these practical principles."

Dwayne Pickett, Pastor,
New Jerusalem Baptist Church, Jackson, Mississippi

"My son, Gary Hawkins presents practical, cutting edge strategies for the church to become relevant within the communities we serve, and push us into fulfilling the kingdom mandate."

Bishop Eddie L. Long, Pastor,
New Birth Missionary Baptist Church, Lithonia, Georgia

"*Marketing Your Church for Growth* is a very concise, practical book that you won't be able to put down if you see that we have got to become all things to all people that by all means we might win some." The ideas for marketing your church are numerous, practical and proven by what God has done at Voices of Faith Ministries."

Rev. Sid Hopkins, Executive Director,
Gwinnett Metro Baptist Association, Lawrenceville, Georgia

"Pastor Gary Hawkins is one of a kind. He has taken marketing to a whole new level when it comes to marketing the Church. His leadership skills are purpose driven. I have read many books, but not one like this. This book must be read by all pastors and leaders. It is practical, thought provoking and a useful tool for pastors who want to lead their church into the 21st century. Exposure is the key and Pastor Hawkins has exposed his ministry through various avenues. This is evident by his tremendous growth. If we are to lead our churches into the 21st century we must think outside the box. Pastor Hawkins has done that. Marketing is the key to bringing exposure to your ministry."

Dr. Larry D. Manning, Bishop,
New Life Baptist Church, Valdosta, Georgia

"Pastor Hawkins has demonstrated to us through his leadership and teachings how to apply Godly entrepreneurship. In his book, *"Marketing Your Church for Growth"* he has helped us to grow spiritually. Because of his keen insights, our business has soared to a higher level. We highly recommend every entrepreneur to read this book and receive a blessing."

Gregory and Betty Levett, Owners,
Gregory B. Levett and Sons Funeral Home, Inc.
Decatur and Scottdale, Georgia

"Pastor Hawkins' practical, yet cutting edge, book takes away every excuse that can be offered for not having a thriving church. Read this book and discover strategies that will establish your church in the community you serve. What Pastor Hawkins shares can extend the reach of your ministry beyond any boundaries that would seek to contain the gospel we preach."

Andre Landers, Senior Pastor,
New Birth South Metropolitan Church, Jonesboro, Georgia

"God has given you an awesome gift and you have made yourself available in the service of the Lord exalting Him and others."

Thomas Ashford, Pastor,
New Jerusalem Missionary Baptist Church, East Point, Georgia

"Pastor Gary Hawkins, Sr. is a gifted, insightful communicator who has written a critically important book. Reading this book is like getting a new prescription for your outdated glasses, allowing you to see the full manifestation of God's hand on his life. If you are looking to take your business to higher grounds, this book is just what you need to get you there."

Stefan Gresham, President and CEO,
Floors with Dimensions, Inc. and GPR Aviation Interiors, Inc.
Atlanta, Georgia

"Once again my brother you have demonstrated the power of God at work in your personal ministry. I pray that every pastor would take a moment and view the jewels that are expressed in this writing. Many have and will continue to call you a pastor of the pastor. The ideas expressed in this book are so real. They represent life changing ministry for all who possess a sincere desire for the continued expansion of the Kingdom of God."

Christopher Chappell, Pastor,
Grace Community Baptist Church, Marietta, Georgia

"As Pastors we are responsible for impacting our communities with the Gospel and for adding people to our churches. In other terms, we are responsible for marketing our churches. Until now, very little has been written from a professional and practical standpoint of view. Pastor Hawkins has done a marvelous job at merging Biblical principle, personal experience, and professional marketing concepts to create a strategy that any pastor any where can use to correctly and effectively market their church. I highly recommend this book and the ideas that are presented."

Randy Clark, Pastor,
Triumph Church of Southeast Texas

"*Marketing Your Church For Growth*" is not just a handbook for churches; it is an excellent tool for business owners, aspiring entrepreneurs and non-profit organizations seeking to soar to new heights. The godly principles and strategies that Pastor Gary Hawkins, Sr. has outlined in this book has helped "On Common Ground News" to become one of the fastest-growing community newspapers in the metro-Atlanta area. A dynamic teacher and thinker, Pastor Hawkins offers fresh insight and inspiration on ways to reach, build and grow."

Glenn and Valerie Morgan, Publishers,
On Common Ground News, Dekalb County, Georgia

"The apostle Paul shared that he was willing to use every tool necessary to win the lost with the gospel (1 Corinthians 9:22). Pastor Gary Hawkins incarnates Paul's words by putting into practice timeless, profound, compelling, life-changing, and transforming information. This book is a priceless gift for anyone in church life or business life, willing to take a risk to fulfill their purpose and walk in their destiny (Ephesians 1:11). Pastor Gary Hawkins uses Kingdom principles to help churches and businesses alike to develop their strategies for reaching people through his God-given ministry of excellence."

Getties L. Jackson, Sr., Senior Pastor,
United Christian Ministries, Greer, South Carolina

"God has placed an awesome gift in my friend, Pastor Gary Hawkins, Sr. This man possesses a spirit of excellence that can surely be admired. "Marketing Your Church for Growth" is a great tool for ministries as well as businesses. Pastor Hawkins and I have had long conversations concerning marketing, and I have been a student to his teachings, and began implementing his God giving insight into our business, and the growth has been amazing. We are witnesses to what God has done in his life and the Voices of Faith Ministries."

Mark and Letecia Miles, Owners,
Miles Photography Studio, Baton Rouge, Louisiana

"Pastor Gary Hawkins offers to the body of Christ and its leadership revelatory insight not only for church growth, but most importantly for reaching the masses for Christ. It is imperative for the 21st century church to remain on the cutting edge of technology and began to do the things that the church has been historically reluctant to do in the way of Marketing the Church. This book will stimulate insightful thinking among church leadership and will totally revolutionize the present church paradigm and refocus the vision of the church toward a kingdom agenda."

Tony D. Cobbins, Senior Pastor,
Canaan Missionary Baptist Church, Kansas City, Missouri

"Pastor Hawkins, I have watched you grow from infancy in ministry, to achieve a level of maturity that very few men and women of God are blessed to achieve. When we speak of blessed people of God, there is no doubt in my mind where you stand on that list. "Marketing Your Church For Growth" is God ordained. If you are serious about building up the kingdom of God, this book gives you the necessary tools to make it happen."

Kiplon L. Taylor, Author,
"A Look Into The Heart of God's Servant", San Diego, California

Marketing

Your Church
For Growth

Marketing

Your Church
For Growth

Reaching and Discipling the
Unchurched with Love and Simplicity

by
GARY HAWKINS, SR.

Published for
GARY HAWKINS MINISTRIES

NILES, ILLINOIS

Dedication

This book is dedicated to God who gave me the vision. I am grateful to my spiritual fathers, Bishop Eddie Long and Pastor William Sheals whose leadership and training has elevated me to this level.

This book is also dedicated to pastors and leaders who are struggling in their faith to grow a great church for God.

I am also dedicating this book to my beautiful wife, and partner in ministry, Debbie E. Hawkins. Through her love and commitment she has joined me in kingdom work for God. This book is also dedicated to my four children, Elaina, Ashley, Gary, Jr., and Kalen. Thank you for your patience and love.

Finally, this book is dedicated to my lovely mother, Mary Louise Robertson. Thank you for keeping me humble when I experience success and encouraged when I fail.

Contents

Acknowledgments

Although God gave me the vision to write this book, writing a book is never a solo effort. Many people worked behind the scenes to make this book become a reality. I would like to sincerely thank many of the individuals who suffered through the labor pains with me in the birthing of this book.

I am grateful for my anointed wife, Debbie, who encourages me to reach for the stars and comforts me when I fall short. She is truly the wind beneath my wings. To my children; Elaina, Ashley, Gary, Jr., and Kalen, you are the best! You constantly remind me how blessed I am.

I am extremely grateful for my mother, Mary Louise Robertson, on whose shoulders I have been privileged to stand. Everything I am or ever hope to be, it is because I stand on the love of my mother's shoulders. To my mother-n-love, Elzina Owens, God has smiled on me sending you into my life. Your love and prayers are unmatched. I am grateful to my aunt, Geraldine Bell, for holding up my mother's arms in prayer when she became weary. I am grateful to my uncle, Ira Bell Jr., for paving the road for our success. To my dad, Aaron Hawkins, Sr., I praise God for our family reunion.

To my brother and sister-n-love, Aaron and Mia Hawkins, no one does it better than the two of you. Your unwavering love and commitment has been unsurpassed. To the rest of my family, Walter, John, Reginald, Denita,

Wayne, Aldreamer, Mary, Warren, Victorina, Chris, Theresa, Gladys, Ann, Gail, Shelia, Dwight, Andrea, Michael, Roy, and Judy, God could not have sent a more loving family. To Earl, Jasper, Paula, and Tyrone, I love you too!

To Mark and Letecia Miles, you have witnessed every major victory and defeat in my life, thanks for your undying friendship. To my nieces, nephews, cousins, and friends, too many to name, you know I love you!

To my executive assistants, Angia Levels and Valerie Murkison, I would not trade you for all the tea in China. Your commitment to excellence continues to push me to the next level. To Lorraine Dykes, where have you been all my life? Thanks for keeping me grounded. To the rest of the staff and members at Voices of Faith, I love you tremendously!

I am also very grateful for the editing assistance of Valerie Morgan, too. Someday I will learn the rules related to hyphens, commas, and semicolons. But not this week.

Finally, this book was written for pastors and leaders who have been called by God to grow a great church. My desire is that the material contained in this book be a blessing to those who implement it.

Pastor Gary Hawkins, Sr.
Voices of Faith Ministries
Stone Mountain, Georgia

Foreword

The church today often fails to be strategic in fulfilling the commission of Christ. We worry about dealing spiritually while sacrificing the practical truths of reaching people. Unlike the days of old, we must aggressively seek to engage the systems of this world and fight battles in arenas that the church of even 20 years ago did not have to fight. The world understands people sometimes better than we do. The world seems to deal with change more effectively also. So, our challenge is to expose and reveal Christ in a society that is changing at a rapid rate. In the early 90's, the United States formed a coalition of nations to fight against Iraq in Desert Storm. The battle was a total victory because of technological changes in the weapons and tactics. The outcome would have been very different if we would have gone into Desert Storm with World War II weapons and tactics. This is a picture of the church today. We are fighting a 2003 cosmic battle with 1950 tactics; the church has become the bane of society because it fails to be relevant. My son, Gary Hawkins presents practical, cutting edge strategies for the church to become relevant within the communities we serve, and push us into fulfilling the kingdom mandate. Some may label him as aberrant or heretical because he ties corporate marketing and business strategies to church growth. But, he is right on point. We must begin to get out of the box we have placed ourselves in and attempted to place

God in, and truly begin to meet people where they are. We must prepare relevant messages and effective ministry. But the question is, "What good is a message for the world and ministry for the nations, if no one is there to be blessed by them?" We are the only fishermen who tell the fish when, where and what to bite, then we complain because no one comes to our churches. Coca Cola does not have that problem; neither does Nike, Microsoft, Las Vegas casinos or any number of other entities. Now we the church...must practically and strategically "market" ourselves for multiplied growth.

Bishop Eddie L. Long, Senior Pastor
New Birth Missionary Baptist Church
Lithonia, Georgia

Introduction

A couple of years ago I was teaching my two boys, Gary, Jr. and Kalen, how to ride a bicycle. They were seven and six years old at the time. Everyday I would take them out to teach them how to ride, but I had no success. Weeks passed and yet they were not riding on their own. I am very protective of my sons. I would hold onto the bicycle while trying to teach them how to balance and pedal on their own. There was one problem, I would not let go of the handle bars.

One Thanksgiving, my family and I drove to Beaumont, Texas to spend the holiday with my mother-n-love, Elzina Owens. My sons were in the yard playing with their cousins, while I was touring the city. When I returned, my two sons were riding on their own. I was absolutely stunned! I approached them and asked, "Who taught you how to ride?" Both of them responded, "Jay!" Jay is my twelve year old nephew. I approached Jay and asked, "How did you teach the boys to ride?" He said, "Uncle Gary, I pushed them and let go." I asked, "All you did was push them and let go?" Being the overprotective dad that I am, I asked, "What happened when they fell?" Jay responded, "Uncle Gary, I picked them back up, pushed and let go again."

I pray that through your reading of this remarkable book, you are pushed to let go of the handle bars (tradition, fear, depression, etc...) that are preventing you from growing a great church for God. Pedal your way safely to the destiny God has chosen for your life. This book is designed to stretch your imagination with practical marketing concepts for the 21st century. It takes you outside-the-box where some of you may feel uncomfortable going, but you will discover that it's where God is.

Chapter One

Marketing Creates Exposure

Marketing is the new buzz word for the 21st century church. If we are going to grow a great church for God, we must meet the unchurched where they are and change our mindset to their way of thinking. We are living in a different time and society than our parents. If we are going to reach our cities and communities, we can no longer conduct church as usual. We must bring exposure to our church through marketing.

The unchurched will never visit our place of worship uninvited.

The unchurched will never visit our place of worship uninvited. We must take the Gospel of Jesus Christ to them. The unchurched will pass our church a thousand times and never notice we exist. Their eyes are not trained to see our church. On many occasions, I've invited an unchurched person to my place of worship, giving them directions to our ministry only to be told, "I pass that location every day, I did not know a church was on that street."

The unchurched does not look for churches to attend. Jesus was very much aware of this concept. In **Matthew 9:9-12**, Jesus approached an unchurched man named Matthew as he was sitting down at the tax office and commanded him to drop what he was doing and follow Him. Jesus knew He had to be the aggressor in order to reach the unchurched.

On the other hand, you will never have to advertise with people who have a relationship with God. They will find you. God is continually on their mind. Even if they relocate to a new city, they will visit several churches until they feel led to join one of them. This concept did not escape Jesus! I am reminded of Nicodemus in **John 3:2** approaching Jesus at night saying, *"...Rabbi, we know that thou art a teacher come from God: for no man can do these miracles that thou doest, except God be with him."* It suggests that Nicodemus was watching Jesus closely and heard about and witnessed the many miracles He performed. Nicodemus being a religious man did not wait to get invited, but in this case he was the aggressor.

WHY PLACE BUSINESSES WITHIN THE CHURCH?

Placing businesses within the church is an effective marketing tool. It gives you an opportunity to bring people into your church who might not attend a Sunday Worship Service.

Voices of Faith has an array of ministry businesses which extends ministry beyond the pulpit. We have a *dance studio, hair salon, barbershop; nail salon, hot tubs in the men and women's bathrooms, a Kids Zone, a fitness center and a 1,600-seat sanctuary* all within our 40,000-square-foot Family Life Center. All of these extend ministry to the unchurched. I know that a lot of you are not comfortable with this kind of ministry, but we truly think outside the box in reaching the unchurched. Remember, the name of the game is exposure! We must expose Christ to the world.

I am convinced that we can no longer be one dimensional in the Body of Christ. We must be able to offer options to the unchurched. Corporate America discovered, after being caught with their pants down during the mid-1980's when all the oil refinery plants went belly up, they could no longer place all their money and trust in one business venture. They had all of their eggs in one basket. Now Fortune 500 companies are multi-dimensional. For example, The Tricon Global Restaurant Company owns Pizza Hut, Taco Bell, and Kentucky Fried Chicken. Arthur Blank, the owner of the Atlanta Falcons Football Team, is also the founder and owner of The Home Depot. Cox Enterprises owns Cox Newspapers (includes The Atlanta Journal-Constitution), Cox Broadcasting, Cox Radio, and the majority owner of Cox

> **We must be able to offer options to the unchurched.**

Communications (Cox Cable, Cox Digital TV). AOL Time Warner Incorporated owns the world's largest internet service provider (America Online); Warner Brothers; Time Magazine; TV channels HBO, CNN and Cartoon Network; Time Warner Cable; and record company Warner Music. AOL Time Warner also owns Turner Entertainment, which includes the Atlanta Braves, Atlanta Hawks, Atlanta Thrashers, Turner Sports, Good Will Games, and the Philips Arena in Atlanta, Georgia.

If one business venture fails, there are other businesses prospering to sustain the company's assets. America Online and Time Warner Inc. merged on January 10, 2000. Three years later, AOL has been plagued by slowing subscriber growth, a fall in advertisement revenue of more than 40 percent, and accounting troubles that are the target of federal criminal investigations. In the first quarter of 2002, AOL Time Warner recorded a $54 billion write-down. Analysts say the company's stock dropped from over $50 per share to as low as $8.70. The company is being sustained by its old media businesses.

Our vision is "to reach and disciple the unchurched with love and simplicity."

Thinking outside the box with our businesses empowers the members of Voices of Faith economically. Another advantage in placing businesses inside the church is community involvement. Businesses inside your church encourage people in the community to visit you. It may be the only time the unchurched steps foot in your church. There is a television in every room of our building. We show videos of our worship service throughout the day. For example, in the hair salon, you are able to watch a broadcast from a previous Sunday morning worship service.

Let me tell you, this marketing concept really works! You've got to know the vision for what God called you to do. Our vision is *"to reach and disciple the unchurched with love and simplicity."* We are truly seeking the unchurched to help bring them into the full knowledge and understanding of God.

Can you think of some businesses that will attract the unchurched to your ministry?
Write some of them here:

1._____

2._____

3._____

4._____

5._____

6._____

7._____

WHY MARKET YOUR CHURCH?

For three years, Voices of Faith Ministries has applied this marketing concept and have grown from 75 members to more than 3,000. This could not have been done without the hand of God on our ministry. I believe we must put ourselves in position for the Glory of God to shine. Jesus tells us in **Matthew 28:18-20** to go and tell the world of His goodness. This is known as "The Great Commission." Jesus Christ is the product. The church is the salesperson. The world is the audience. If we are to get our product in the homes of the unchurched, we must aggressively pursue and promote Christ to the world. We cannot sit back anymore and place a marquee outside our church and expect people to show up because we are open for worship service. Those days are history.

> **Jesus Christ is the product. The church is the salesperson. The world is the audience.**

Flooding the market with Jesus Christ and promoting our church's name is the most important reason for marketing our ministries. Billboards, fliers, radio, television, magazines, newspapers, are just a few of the ways to market your church.

Never let the unchurched forget who you are. McDonald's and Coca Cola ads are shown everywhere. They are at every sporting event, concert, and they are seen across the globe. They spend billions of dollars each year promoting their products. McDonald's and Coca

Cola doesn't advertise because we are not aware of their business; they advertise so we don't forget who they are. They understand the value of advertising. Don't ever let them forget about who you are.

If you want people to know your name and to know you exist, you must flood the market with creative promotional tools that will attract the attention of the unchurched. The gurus of marketing say a person must see your name at least 19 times before they even know that you exist. We no longer can just show up and preach the Gospel of Jesus Christ; we must effectively market God's church. There are numerous preachers in the body of Christ. What is causing your church to stand out from others? Great preaching doesn't grow great churches for God; great leaders do. Some of the most dynamic preachers in the world have fewer than 50 members attending Sunday worship. As a matter of fact, the average church in America has 75 members and it has reached its plateau.

Often times we are frustrated when we see mega churches growing by leaps and bounds. The first question that comes to mind is why his church growing and mine isn't? We often feel we are the better preacher. I can hear you now saying you can preach rings around Reverend Butterfly's head, but preaching is only one tool needed to pastor a growing congregation. Mega churches expose themselves to the community with their community-minded events. I remember when New Birth Missionary Baptist Church, one of the largest churches in America, was in the early stages of growth in the early 1990's in the city of Atlanta. My father in the ministry, Bishop Eddie L. Long, New Birth's pastor, was once quoted as saying, "If a pin drops in the city of Atlanta, someone from New Birth needed to be there to pick it up." Exposure!

Let me set the record straight, it is very important to have a well-prepared message to bless the people who are coming for a fresh word, but preaching is not the only common denominator that can affect church growth.

Voices of Faith Ministries has been ordained by God to take over the city of Atlanta, the state of Georgia, America, and eventually the world for Jesus Christ. This is my mindset. How am I going to do it? Billboards have been strategically placed all over the city of Atlanta, Georgia. We are in local newspapers (On Common Ground News), and we're on television broadcasting locally and nationwide. Voices of Faith Ministries is only 8 years old. The city must know we exist. We can't just put a church sign up and say, "I'm here, come and worship with us." Today more than ever, much more is needed.

HOW MUCH WILL IT COST?

This is one of the most crucial areas of marketing. Spend only what your budget will allow. Don't try to keep up with the Jones'. Spend only what you can afford. When we started Voices of Faith Ministries 8 years ago, we did not have the money to broadcast on television and we did not have money to advertise on billboards. We only had enough money to pass out fliers in the community and shopping centers. My wife, Debbie, and I, along with our four children, would go door to door throughout the community inviting people to visit our church. To this day, there are still people who approach me saying how they remember us stopping by their homes ministering to them. After handing out fliers, I would sometimes drive back through the neighborhoods and shopping centers and I would notice several fliers on the ground. The people would immediately throw them away. Guess what? I expected that to happen. Our church had no credibility. They did not know who we were.

Spend only what you can afford.

People will never come visit your church without credibility. The fliers were slowly bringing exposure and credibility to our ministry. There are lots of creative marketing ideas that cost very little. You just have to think outside of the box. I remember being in a city visiting and I saw members of a church on a corner at a busy red light passing out cold sodas with their church name wrapped around the can. No strings attached. They did not invite them to church. They did not ask for money. They only said, "May God bless you!" They were bringing exposure to their ministry. People often times are turned off by churches always asking for money. In this case, the church was passing out blessings. What do you think happened next? The people said, "I must visit your church because you are totally different from other ministries." Exposure is the name of the game.

WHY TARGET THE SCHOOLS?

Why target the schools in your area? Educators need the Lord too, don't they? The schools are perfect areas to witness for the Lord. Don't go to the schools asking what they can do for you, rather what your church can contribute to them. This is one of my favorite areas of marketing because you often see immediate results. Children bring their parents to church. As a matter of fact, we have a policy that allows children to participate in any ministry in the church without being a member. We do this for one reason: Children will recruit their parents. Parents must join before participating in ministry because we need total commitment. The higher you set standards in your church, the better quality of people will be attracted to your ministry.

The higher you set standards in your church, the better quality of people will be attracted to your ministry.

God gave me a tremendous vision to reach our children through the school system. The impact has been tremendous! We initially targeted two high schools, one from Gwinnett County, Georgia and the other from DeKalb County, Georgia. Voices of Faith Ministries is located in Stone Mountain, Georgia in Gwinnett County, and on the border of DeKalb County. Fifty percent of our membership lives in Gwinnett County, and forty seven percent lives in DeKalb County. After meeting with the principals of the two schools, we are allowed to minister to the students during their lunch hours. My staff goes over to the schools weekly sharing Christ and offering assistance wherever necessary. Several of the high school kids from each school have visited us on many occasions. As a matter of fact, our kids from Voices of Faith help lead other students to Christ. Our teenagers have played a major role in encouraging unchurched students to visit and join our ministry. Oftentimes, our teenagers are escorting their classmates to the altar for salvation. The results are awesome! We also assist the schools' administration staff with counseling and security for athletic events.

We implemented a Community Service Program with the Schools call Project H.O.P.E. (Helping Other People Excel). When a student gets suspended for three days, he/she can come to Voices of Faith and participate in community work to reduce the suspension to only one day. The schools loved the idea because they know most kids who are suspended are home alone and find themselves getting into deeper trouble. Project H.O.P.E. also assist with tutoring, on-the-job training, interview techniques, and other community service programs. Once again, we have brought exposure to our ministry through helping the schools.

In Georgia, there are several Teacher Work days allocated for faculty development. The students are given those days off. Whenever there are Teacher Work days, the cafeteria does not provide breakfast or lunch. We approached about 5 schools in the area and catered lunch to the faculty and staffs for the work teachers do all year. Place a sign or banner in the cafeteria letting the staff know the food was compliments of your ministry. We also send several staff members to the luncheon to represent the church. We get an opportunity to get instant feedback on their gratitude. The results are powerful! Recently, one of the schools whom we catered lunch wanted to thank us by attending our 11:00 a.m. Sunday worship service on January 26, 2003. We blocked off over 200 seats to accommodate the staff and their families. We introduced the principal and her entire staff to our congregation. This created tremendous exposure for our ministry. Steve Sjogren, author of "101 Ways To Reach Your Community" said, "As we serve people who don't know Christ, they're automatically curious. It's only natural for them to ask, "So, why are you doing this?" In this age of selfishness, it's startling for someone to do a deed of kindness with no apparent strings attached." 1 Peter 3:15 says, *"But sanctify the Lord God in your hearts: and be ready always to give an answer to every man that asketh you a reason of the hope that is in you with meekness and fear."*

On January 22, 2003, we received a telephone call from the principal of Lithonia High School in Lithonia, Georgia asking to use our facility for their 2003 Baccalaureate ceremony on May 18, 2003 at 3:00 p.m. A Baccalaureate ceremony is a farewell address in the form of a sermon delivered to a graduating class. The principal asked me to be their keynote speaker. Tremendous exposure!

Recently, the DeKalb County School Board called us and asked if they could use our facility to hold their annual "Teacher of the Year Program" at our church. Our facility was chosen because of our community involvement. This program honored 100 teachers from various schools for their outstanding work. I was chosen to be the keynote speaker. I was elated! After praising God for the opportunity, the next thought came to my mind: Exposure! When you go into the school system and expose yourself, it exposes people to your ministry. This is the fruit of the labor of love for God.

Another way of greatly enhancing your ministry is checking with various schools to determine if they need a Chaplain for their sport teams. Let me tell you, I was blessed when one of my members, Stefan Gresham, invited me to a breakfast attended by the Reverend Jesse Jackson of Rainbow Push. There were approximately 200 other guests, corporate sponsors, and local politicians present for the occasion. After fellowshipping for a couple of hours and meeting all kinds of interesting people, I headed for the valet parking to get my car. I noticed a tall man with a familiar face I've seen before on television. It was Paul Hewitt, the basketball coach for the Georgia Tech Yellow Jackets. We engaged in a very lengthy conversation. I told him how I have admired his teams. They all play with great enthusiasm! I asked him would he be interested in me being their Chaplain for his men's basketball team. At first, he was hesitant because he did not know me from Adam. I had no credibility with him.

However, after talking further, he invited me to have lunch with him to further discuss our future together. One word: Exposure! There are too many churches to choose from: Your ministry is not the only one on the block. What will make your church different? You have to make sure folks know who you are and what you have to offer.

While waiting for my car to arrive, I met the President of Citizens Trust Bank of Atlanta, Georgia. I introduced myself; he stopped me in the middle of my introduction and said, "Pastor Hawkins, I know who you are! Your pictures, along with your church, are plastered on billboards all over the city of Atlanta. I also watch your weekly television broadcast. One of my good

Great preaching doesn't grow great churches; leadership does.

friends, Mr. Gregory Levett of Levett and Sons Funeral Home is a member of your church." He went on to ask if I would consider utilizing his bank when we build our next facility. He agreed to handle the deal himself.

Are you getting the picture? Exposure! Our growth has been strategically done, it is not by accident. Great preaching doesn't grow great churches; leadership does. I personally know too many pastors who can break a word down into tiny pieces. I have seen them dissect the word, grill it, boil it, bake it and yet nothing of significance is happening because of their lack of leadership skills and marketing ability.

Can you think of schools in your area that would benefit from your ministry's involvement?

List some of them here:

1._____

2._____

3._____

4._____

5._____

6._____

7._____

BIG BROTHER/BIG SISTER MENTORING PROGRAM

One area of immediate impact is the Big Brother/Big Sister Mentoring Program. This is a hands-on approach to ministry. You not only get an opportunity to mentor a child, but it's also an opportunity to bring stability into his or her life. If there were an abundance of Big Brother/Big Sister Mentoring Programs in our school systems, most of them would be a healthy environment for our children to learn and excel. In order to go to the next level with our children, it takes a village to get them there. We have already seen a tremendous impact with the children who are in our program. It truly works!

For Discussion

1. Why is it so important to market your church in the 21st century?

2. What effects can businesses have in your ministry?

3. What is the average size church in America?

4. Why is it important to measure the cost before advertising?

5. Do you feel targeting the schools in your area are effective? Explain.

6. How do you feel about Big Brother/Big Sister Mentoring Programs? Explain.

7. Why is it important to be multi-dimensional in the church?

Chapter Two

Great Growth Ideas!

TELEVISION

Television reaches more people at one time than any other media outlet. No other media outlets compare to television. Television gives the unchurched an opportunity to look into your ministry without actually being there. Often times, the unchurched will not visit churches because they don't want to feel pressured into joining before they decide where they want

> **Television reaches more people at one time than any other media outlet.**

to call home. Today, a lot of people are afraid to attend church because of hurt and neglect from previous pastors and members in the congregation.

Our television broadcast has played a major role in our ministry in reaching the unchurched. There are so many different people in all walks of life that approach me everyday to tell me they are watching the broadcast. I receive letters and e-mails from all across the country from unchurched people getting to know Jesus Christ as their personal Savior through our broadcast. I cannot tell you the number of letters I have received from prison inmates all over this country telling me about our broadcast and how it has been a blessing to them. Television brings instant exposure and credibility.

The cost of television can become very pricey if you don't have the proper equipment and have not done your research in the industry. There are lots of decisions that have to be made before launching your television ministry. Selecting the right cameras and editing equipment are very important. Cameras vary in prices. There are some digital cameras that you can purchase for as low as $3,000 per camera. Cameras with excellent quality costs from as low as $3,000 to as high as $100,000. Used cameras are also excellent for broadcasting your ministry. A pastor friend of mine in the Atlanta area goes to Las Vegas for a camera show each year. He purchases used cameras that are still in excellent condition for his television broadcast.
Deciding whether or not you want to outsource your editing or edit your broadcast in house will depend on your current situation. The cost to outsource your editing can become very expensive. The average editor in the city of Atlanta charges about $500 per 30-minute broadcast. If

you decide to edit your broadcast in house, then you must staff the position. If you search through your congregation, you will probably find someone with television or media background or who has a desire to be trained.

The local television access stations in your city may offer to train people for a low cost to operate cameras, edit broadcast and to even produce a show. It is usually a six week course. There are some access stations that allow you to record your broadcast with their equipment for free once you have completed the six week training seminar.

The last stage is airing your broadcast. Once you have decided which camera to use and who will edit the broadcast, the next step is finding the right cities you want to air your broadcast. Depending on what city and what television station you choose to air your broadcast, you could spend anywhere

Everyone sees the billboards.

from as low as $30 per 30 minute broadcast to as much as $20,000 per 30 minute broadcast. Even though television can be the most expensive way to promote your ministry to the world, it also brings the greatest exposure to the unchurched.

BILLBOARDS

Billboards bring great exposure to your ministry! Everyone sees the billboards. Billboards don't discriminate. Everyone, no matter the color, creed, gender, or race, will see your billboards during their drive time. Whether a person is a member of a church or an atheist, your billboard will attract attention.

We have approximately six billboards across the city of Atlanta. Billboards are one of the best methods of promoting your product. A billboard is seen 24 hours a day 7 days a week. In my opinion, billboards make a statement unlike any other form of advertisement. It says to the people we are different and are on the cutting edge of ministry. Ten percent of Voices of Faith visitors each Sunday come from billboards.

Billboards vary in price range. The location of a billboard can determine whether you pay as low as $150 per month to as high as $2,000 per month. The size of the billboard will also determine your cost at the location. The billboard companies base their prices on two things. The first is the size of the billboard. Billboards come in three sizes. The second thing billboard companies base their pricing on is location. The busier the location, the more money you are likely to pay.

The billboard companies also design your graphic art pictures. It is usually associated with a cost. The cost alone to design your ad and place it on the billboard could be approximately $700. If you can afford billboards, I highly recommend them!

What you place on the billboards is very important. The wording should be short and to the point. Too much can take away from your theme. Remember, the motorist are driving at speeds of as much as 55 mph. They only have about 3 to 5 seconds to glance while driving. Here is an example of one of Voices of Faith Ministries' billboards.

BUS STOPS

Bus stop ads are another means of introducing Christ to the unchurched. Bus stop ads are inexpensive and very effective. You should place these ads in strategic places where the masses can see your advertisements.

Bus stop advertising is inexpensive. The cost for a bus stop ad ranges from $50 to $100 per month. I truly like the visibility you get with bus stops.

After graduating from Southern University in Baton Rouge, Louisiana in 1985, I moved to San Diego, California to work for General Dynamics as a Financial

Analyst. I immediately began looking for a church, but there was one major problem, I did not have transportation to get around town. So, I would catch the bus and ride to church on Sunday mornings. Voices of Faith advertises at local bus stops all over the city with amazing results! When the unchurched are sitting and waiting for their buses to arrive, they are able to see our ads.

People tend to go where the action is!

Marketing your ministry will bring great rewards. I tell pastors all the time to rent a bulldozer and place it on the church grounds and watch the excitement it brings to a community. Let the bulldozer turn some dirt up from time to time. People will come by and visit because they think you are doing something powerful. Everyone wants to be part of something that is a success. People tend to go where the action is!

Another powerful tool for marketing your church is placing an ad directly on the bus. Again, this is low budget advertising with great results. Wherever the bus travels, your church is being promoted. This will allow you to go places you don't ordinarily travel. People want to be where folks "got it going on."

RADIO

The radio can be another effective marketing tool for reaching the unchurched. Millions of people a day tune into the radio. The radio can be very expensive. Radio is probably the second most expensive form of advertisement in the media industry. You can pay as low as $75 per week to as high as $300 per week on a 15-minute slot. Although the radio rates can be extremely high, your impact is immediate. Whenever we have done commercials on the radio, we've received many calls from members as well as the unchurched letting us know they heard our radio commercial.

Most of your unchurched will listen to FM.

If you are being led to do radio ministry. I encourage you to look for a popular FM secular station to air your broadcast. Traditionally, churches have aired on AM stations, but the signals are not as strong as FM. Most FM stations have the capability of reaching millions of people at a time. If your goal is to reach the unchurched, it is more effective to reach them on the FM dial. The FM usually has the highest-rated radio broadcast. Most of your unchurched will listen to FM.

ON COMMON GROUND NEWS

On Common Ground News is a local community oriented newspaper that reaches over 50,000 people per month. This is not a church newspaper. Rather, it's a secular newspaper that allows churches to advertise. Utilizing this secular tool has been a tremendous asset to the growth of our membership. This is a great place to advertise upcoming events to your community. We use this newspaper to promote our Easter and Christmas Service, drama plays, musicals, conferences, workshops, and many others.

On Common Ground keeps our communities informed of major and up-to-the minute events taking place in and around our community, as well as our County. Find a local secular newspaper or magazine in your community to advertise. This will be one of your biggest impacts.

HOW ARE THE VISITORS FINDING YOUR CHURCH?

It is crucial to track how visitors are finding your church. Placing a tracking system in your church to monitor visitors is a must. A tracking system lets you know whether or not your church is healthy. Without a tracking system, you cannot effectively determine the health of your church. The next four pages will show the different graphs we use to determine the health of our church. "Exhibit A" shows the marketing tools we use to track how visitors hear about our church. Note the list of marketing tools we use to determine the church's health: Billboards, Television, On Common Ground, Friend, Drive-By, and Other. This is a simple way of tracking visitors to your church. "Exhibit B" shows our total number of visitors and the rapid growth in membership from July 25, 1999 to January

EXHIBIT A
VOICES OF FAITH MINISTRIES
TOTAL MONTHLY VISITORS
October 2002

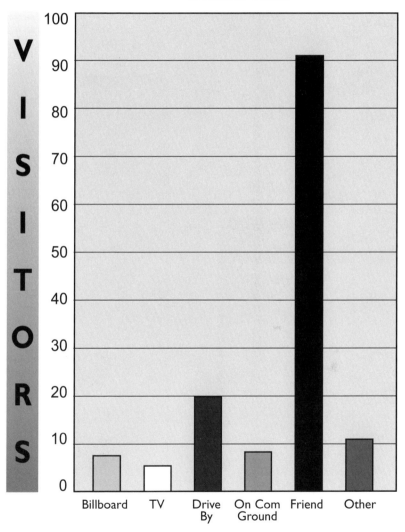

EXHIBIT B
MEMBER STATUS
July 1999 to January 2003

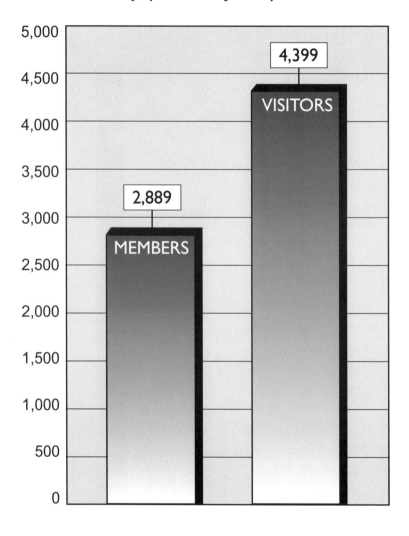

EXHIBIT C

VOICES OF FAITH MINISTRIES
WEEKLY MEMBERSHIP
October 2002

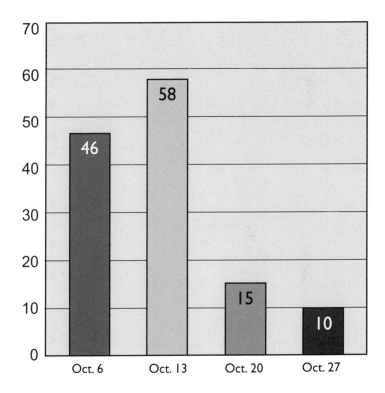

EXHIBIT D
MEMBER RESIDENCE BY COUNTY
January 2003

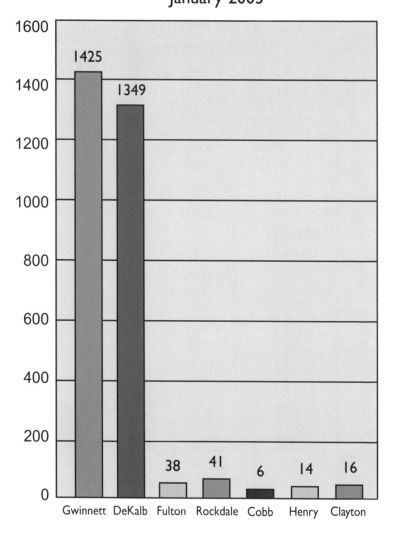

12, 2003. "Exhibit C" shows our weekly membership in October 2002 as a result of marketing. "Exhibit D" identifies the demographics of the membership.

Notice in "Exhibit A" most of our visitors heard about Voices of Faith through a friend or family member. This is the No. 1 marketing tool in the world. It is called "word of mouth". Seventy percent of our visitors are invited to the church by family and friends. Isn't it amazing, for all of the money we invest in marketing, 70 percent of our visitors

Sheep beget sheep.

comes from family and friends inviting them to church? It is an awesome sign when your church members are leading the church in marketing. It suggests that your church is extremely healthy. Sheep beget sheep. If you find a great restaurant where the food is excellent and the hospitality is off the chain, you won't keep it to yourself, but you will call a friend and invite him to the restaurant as well. That is precisely what our church members do when they invite others to church where the spiritual food and the hospitality are wonderful. Sheep have more credibility and trust with other sheep than with a preacher inviting them to church. The people will trust what a friend says rather than a stranger. Using "Exhibit A" keeps you alert and aware of the health in your church.

"Exhibit B" is another tool to keep you informed of your church's health. This graph illustrates the total number of visitors and the rapid growth in membership from July 25, 1999 to January 12, 2003. As you can see from

"Exhibit B", 65.7 percent of our first-time visitors joined our ministry. Those numbers alone are incredible! That means for every two people that visits Voices of Faith, one joined. The national average of first-time visitors joining a church is less than 20 percent. There are other factors that cause people to join your ministry that I will discuss later in this book.

"Exhibit C" shows the church's weekly membership growth in October 2002. "Exhibit C" shows you week by week the number of people joining the ministry. It truly is a strong indicator of the health of your ministry. It also proves that God's hand is upon our ministry and the marketing tools are getting great results.

"Exhibit D" identifies the demographics of the membership. "Exhibit D" breaks down our membership by the counties in which they live. This is very helpful when planning for strategic marketing events. For example, the majority of our membership is in Gwinnett and DeKalb counties. When strategizing for new ideas, Gwinnett and DeKalb counties will be our target market because they comprise the majority of our membership.

MOVIE THEATRES

Movie theatres are a fantastic marketing tool. I truly enjoy the exposure of movie theatres. You are able to reach people of all walks of life. If there are 16 movie screens, you have the opportunity to advertise on 16 screens. If each movie screen shows 4 movies a day, you have the capability of being seen 64 times a day. Great exposure!

One of my members once asked me, "Pastor Hawkins, will you advertise in the "R" rated movies?" I said, "Yes, they need Jesus Christ, too." Remember, our vision at Voices of Faith is "to reach and disciple the unchurched with love and simplicity."

MARQUEE

The marquee sign in front of most churches can be a great marketing tool. You get an opportunity to reach the unchurched daily. There are approximately 30,000 cars per day that pass our church. The marquee informs them of our weekly activities.

Never use your marquee for a "thought for today" sign. You waste a valuable advertising tool. There are a couple of churches in my area I pass everyday that display a "thought for today" on their marquee. I thoroughly enjoy reading it. They are wonderful little antidotes that bless me each time I read them,

Never use your marquee for a "thought for today" sign.

but it has never encouraged me to want to see what was happening in their church. "Thought for today" signs don't lure people to your church, signs that inform the community of activities in your church do.

FAMILY AND FRIENDS DAY

Family and Friends Day is an awesome day to promote the kingdom of God and your ministry. This has been one of my favorite times of the year. The gratification is marvelous!

Each 5th Sunday during the year, we encourage our members to invite people to church to celebrate Family and Friends. We specifically ask each member to invite at least three people which represents the Trinity (Father, Son, Holy Spirit). We also reward the member who invites the most guests. The reward can range from a $100 gift certificate to their favorite grocery store to a dinner for the entire family at their favorite restaurant. On September 29, 2002, we celebrated our 8th annual Family and Friends Day. One of our members had 37 family and friends attend our special Sunday worship. Another member had 32 in attendance. We decided to bless both of them with gift certificates.

Each time we celebrate Family and Friends Day, our church has standing room only. On June 16, 2002, we moved into our new 1,600 seat Family Life Center and on Family and Friends Day our sanctuary was packed.

We encourage each member to purchase a Voices of Faith T-shirt and wear jeans and tennis shoes for their comfort on Family and Friends Day. Our church colors are blue and white. It is a beautiful sight to see your entire congregation in one accord worshipping God and giving Him all the Glory. The great thing about the T-shirts is the exposure Voices of Faith gets when our members wear them to the malls, grocery stores, movie theatres, sporting events and many other places exposing our ministry.

VISITOR CARDS

Visitor Cards, when used effectively, can be a great marketing tool. To many people the visitor's card is worth five cents. To me the visitor's card is worth millions of dollars. Most churches have not totally utilized the information on the card. Your visitor cards must be specifically designed with your vision in mind. Your logo and information should be on the card. I see too many churches using generic visitor cards. It must be catered to your ministry.

To many people the visitor's card is worth five cents. To me the visitor's card is worth millions of dollars.

Take advantage of the information on the card. For instance, anyone who places a check mark on single or married gets a phone call from our singles or couples ministry. If anyone circles ages 50 and over, they get a phone call from our senior ministry. There's a section on our card that list the various ministries. Once they check mark the information on a particular ministry, someone from that ministry follows up with a call. We take advantage of how the visitors hear about our church. We advertise in various places such as billboards, On Common Ground News, television, website, and drive by. For example, if

33

the billboard was checked on the visitor's card, it gives us information on where to put future advertising dollars.

Each visitor who fills out a visitor card and turns it in to one of the gatekeepers (ushers) receives a free audio tape. The impact is instant. The visitors get an opportunity to listen to one of my messages. This encourages them to gain a closer relationship with God and to become part of a fast growing church family.

I personally call each visitor weekly. Voices of Faith averages approximately 60 visitors a week and I take the time to call each one. Keep your conversation short and to the point. Limit your conversation to three minutes or less. Value their time. Express to them your gratitude for taking the time out of their busy schedule to worship with you. Encourage them to visit again.

> **I personally call each visitor weekly.**

I cannot begin to tell you the number of people who joined our church because I took the time to call. Most visitors are so stunned that I called they are usually speechless. Most have said, "I've never had the pastor call my house before. I am extremely impressed." Continue to send letters each week along with calling all visitors yourself. You will see instant results! In our new members' orientation class, we polled our new members to find out what made them join the church. Fifty percent of the people when asked said, "I joined because the pastor called my house." George Barna, author of "Grow Your Church From The Outside In" said, "Unchurched people are more likely to respond to a personal invitation than they are to surrender to pressure to belong to a group."

Look closely at your visitor's card. You are sitting on a gold mine for the Lord. List the number of ways the card can be an effective tool for outreach:

1._____

2._____

3._____

4._____

5._____

RECREATIONAL LEAGUES

Recreational leagues are a great idea for marketing your church. Your church can sponsor a little league baseball or basketball team. The team can wear the church's uniform. Any sports league that involve our children will always attract people from all walks of life. Can you imagine the marketing for your church? When your team hits a home-run or scores a basket, your church's name is mentioned each time over the loud speakers. Great exposure!

LEADERSHIP LUNCHEON

This marketing concept has the ability to supercede all the others. We get the opportunity to affect leaders and entrepreneurs in our community. There are so many businesses struggling to stay afloat. Host a quarterly leadership luncheon at your place of worship. Teach them the biblical principles for a successful business. It will empower the businesses in your communities to develop economical wealth. Every successful business gets its principles from the bible. God is no respecter of persons. The principles are divine. Sponsoring luncheons will create great exposure for your ministry.

Many of these same entrepreneurs may eventually call your church home. It is called the Law of Reciprocity, the more I give, the more it comes back to me. Have the leadership luncheon catered. Ask each entrepreneur to donate $10 for the luncheon.

BIRTH LETTER
OF CONGRATULATIONS

This marketing tool can affect the lives of thousands of people, if done in a spirit of excellence. Each week in the local newspapers, the birth of hundreds of babies are listed. Get the local newspaper and write letters to families who are celebrating the birth of a new born child. Congratulate them on the birth of their child. Let them know the ministries in your church that caters to children. Great exposure!

DEATH LETTERS OF CONDOLENCES

This is another marketing tool that can affect thousands. You need someone to write letters who is sensitive to grieving families. Each day the local newspapers list death notices in the obituary section. Send a letter of condolences letting the grieving family know you are praying for them.

Even though the family may not know your name, you have just blessed them with a personal letter and created exposure for your ministry in the process.

For Discussion

1. Do you feel advertising on television is the most powerful and effective way of promoting the church? Explain.

2. Can billboards attract the unchurched to your ministry? Explain.

3. How are the visitors finding your church?
   Name three ways.

1._____

2._____

3._____

4. How can Family and Friends Day be effective
   in reaching the unchurched?
   Explain.

5. How much is the visitor's card worth to you?
   Explain.

6. Do you feel Recreational leagues are great ideas
   for marketing the church?
   Explain.

7. How effective can a leadership luncheon be in leading
   the unchurched to Jesus Christ?

Chapter Three

Stages of Growth

THREE STAGES OF LEADERSHIP

There are three stages of leadership. First, a pastor must walk with the sheep. Secondly, a pastor must walk ahead of the sheep. Thirdly, a pastor must walk above the sheep. These three stages of leadership are crucial. Mastering them will successfully take you to the next level of ministry. Let's get started:

A pastor must walk with the sheep

This stage of ministry is the most crucial of the three. In this stage, the pastor and his flock must get acquainted with one another. The flock must catch the shepherd's scent. They must actively see the pastor participating in ministry. In this stage, the flock needs to see you getting your hands dirty.

In the beginning stages of our ministry, I probably participated in everything our church had to offer. I ushered, sang in the choir, led out in devotion, and carried and set up the speaker system each week. Our family van doubled as the church van on Sunday. I preached, taught Bible Study and Sunday School. I truly was a jack-of-all trades and a master of none. I will cherish those days the rest of my life.

Your flock has to see you cleaning, dusting, mopping, and taking out the trash. If the church building needs painting, you should be the first to grab a paint brush. If the grass need cutting, beat them to the lawn mower. Once your flock gets your scent, your ministry is ready to go to the next level. Too many pastors skip this stage because they think working with the sheep is beneath them. It is in the fields where the sheep fall in love with its shepherd.

> **Your flock has to see you cleaning, dusting, mopping, and taking out the trash.**

As I said earlier, this is the most crucial of the three stages of growth. After spending valuable time with your sheep, you must sense when its time to move to the next stage of leadership. If you stay too long, they will become too familiar with you. They will no longer see you as Pastor Hawkins, now they see you as

"Gary." Your flock no longer sees the anointing on your life because they have gotten too close to the flesh. You will discover your sermons don't have the same impact as they once did. In Mark 6:1-6, Jesus faced similar problems. He was only able to heal a few of the sick. This was not because He lacked anointing, but because the people were too familiar with His flesh. They remembered Jesus as the little boy of the carpenter, Joseph's son, and Mary's baby.

A pastor must walk ahead of the sheep

The second stage of leadership is just as important as the first stage, but not as crucial. The toughest part for a pastor in this stage is to know when to detach himself/herself from the flock. In order to go to the next level, pastors must walk ahead of the sheep. The sheep has to see you leading by example. They need to see a sermon and not hear one. Your preaching has to be in direct relationship with your faith.

They need to see a sermon and not hear one.

In October 1998, I stood in my pulpit and told my congregation we were going to buy 20 acres of land and build a 6,000 square-foot church. We had only 30 faithful members and 15 of them were children. In the natural, I was committing suicide, but in the supernatural, God was saying, "Bring it on baby!" I had been preaching about the power of God and walking in faith and now the people

41

needed to see my faith. More than ever, they needed to see a sermon.

I told my congregation I did not know how God was going to provide, but God was going to prompt someone to bless us with enough money to build His church. The cost of our project was $750,000. The bank gave us 90 days to raise $100,000 as a down payment. We started asking friends and loved ones to contribute toward this momentous task. Now remember, we only had 15 adults. We are part of the Georgia Baptist Convention. The Georgia Baptist Convention has a policy that, "If you purchase 7 acres or less, they will lend you $15,000 toward the purchase of your land. If you purchase 8 acres or more, they will lend you $25,000." We were purchasing 20 acres. I approached the Stone Mountain Association of the Georgia Baptist Convention to inquire about the loan. To make a long story short, I was turned down. The association did not feel we were a strong enough church to handle the debt. I understood their reasoning, but God's hand was on me for a greater work. I resigned from the association. I knew if our church was going to get to the next level, I had to rid myself of any negative vibes.

Two weeks earlier, I was up at 2:00 a.m. studying the blueprint of our future church when the Holy Spirit spoke to me. "Gary, open the yellow pages and call this church and make an appointment with the pastor." Later that morning, I called the church and made the appointment with the pastor. I knew absolutely nothing about the church. I was obedient to God.

Two weeks later, I received a phone call from the church secretary reminding me of my appointment the next morning with the pastor I was meeting. I asked for directions because I had no idea where I was going or who I was meeting. I was just being obedient to God. The pastor and I enjoyed a wonderful lunch together. I shared the vision God gave me and poured out my heart to him concerning ministry. He asked, "Gary, have you ever thought about joining the Georgia Baptist Convention." In my mind, I said, "Lord, you brought me out here to get insulted again!" I explained that they had recently turned me down for a loan of $25,000 and I was no longer associated with the Convention. He picked up his cell phone and called the Georgia Baptist Convention. He introduced himself and said, "I want you to cut a check for $25,000 for my good friend Gary Hawkins, Sr., pastor of Voices of Faith Ministries in Stone Mountain. He is about to do a great work for God." After praising God and regaining my composure, I asked, "Who are you to call and get the Georgia Baptist Convention to write a check to us for $25,000?" He said, "You don't know who I am?" I said, "No sir." He said, "I am the president of the Georgia Baptist Convention." His name is Frank Cox, pastor of North Metro Baptist Church, one of the largest churches in the state of Georgia. We were immediately encouraged by Sid Hopkins, Executive Director of the Gwinnett Metro Baptist Association to join their association. Joining the association has been one of the best moves our church has made. Sid has been an awesome role model for helping churches to grow. The Georgia Baptist Convention asked the Gwinnett Metro Baptist Association to write the check for $25,000 to us.

Friends and love ones all over the United States started sending money to bless the work of God. Two of the first people to respond were celebrities; Blair Underwood, actor and Todd Kinchens, Atlanta Falcons Wide Receiver. I remember getting a letter from Todd Kinchens saying, "Pastor Hawkins, when I looked into your eyes and saw the picture of your family, I knew God was about to do a great work in your life." Needless to say, when the dust cleared, $103,000 was collected in 90 days. Praise God! Don't be afraid to dream! John Maxwell, author of "Failing Forward" said, "To achieve your dreams, you must embrace adversity and make failure a regular part of your life. If you're not failing, you're probably not really moving forward."

Money always follows movement!

The sheep has to see you leading by example. They need to see a sermon and not hear one. As they see your faith in action, their faith will increase as well. Money always follows movement!

A pastor must walk above the sheep

The final stage is equally important as the first two stages of leadership. In this stage, the vision for your ministry is cast. In order to build a mega church, leadership becomes a priority. There are no Lone Rangers in this stage. A pastor has to be able to equip his leaders to lead others to the next level. You will never grow a great church for God without the help of great leaders around you!

> **The learning curve of life and leadership will humble the strongest of men.**

A pastor must delegate authority in this stage of ministry. We must give our leaders an opportunity to succeed through trial and error. I grew as a pastor through my failures. The learning curve of life and leadership will humble the strongest of men. It was in my failures that I became weak, but God became strong.

FOUR LEVELS OF CHURCH GROWTH

The Horse and Buggy Stage

The Horse and Buggy Stage of church growth is where most churches congregate. This stage has less than 200 members. The average church in America has 75 members. This stage is usually your church family members passing down tradition from one generation to another. The Horse and Buggy Stage has members who have sat in the same seat in the sanctuary for over 25 years. The pastor does it all in this stage.

I am reminded of my former pastor in San Diego, California who visited a church in Los Angeles where he was scheduled to preach. Before service began, he sat in the audience to get a view of the sanctuary. An elderly gentleman walked up to him and said, "Sir, you are sitting in my chair. My father sat in this same chair and his father before him. This chair is passed down from generation to generation." This stage has very few leaders.

Crab-In-The-Bucket Stage

The Crab-in-the-bucket Stage of church growth is where everyone knows everyone. This stage has approximately 200 - 400 members. With this crab-in-the-bucket mentality, this stage doesn't want to add new people to the church. They are very traditional. The Crab-in-the-bucket Stage is very comfortable in its present environment. They like things simple and they resist change.

Water Cooler Stage

The Water Cooler Stage of church growth is when the church starts reaching people through evangelizing. This stage has approximately 400 - 800 members. At this stage, the people in your city start recognizing your name. Word of mouth is spreading rapidly about your church. The unchurched starts hearing about your ministry at the water cooler at work.

The "ER" Stage

The Emergency Room (ER) Stage of church growth causes your church to rethink how ministry is operated. We must be quick thinkers on our feet. This stage has over 800 members. Churches can no longer be run by the pastor only in this stage. Entrepreneurs and political leaders are interested in being part of your ministry.

Elmer Towns, C. Peter Wagner, and Thom S. Rainer, authors of "The Everychurch Guide to Growth" said, "Growth is the most dynamic thing in life. Life is a gift of God to the farmer who grows crops. Life is the gift of God to parents who raise a baby, and life is a gift to pastors who lead a church. Growth means life, energy, new horizons, new freedoms, and new attainments. Growth means the fulfillment of expectations."

For Discussion

1. What are the three stages of leadership?

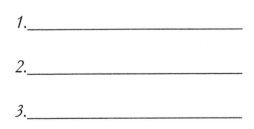

1. _____

2. _____

3. _____

2. *Why is it important for a pastor to walk with the sheep? Explain.*

3. *Why is it important for a pastor to walk ahead of the sheep? Explain.*

4. *Why is it important for a pastor to walk above the sheep? Explain.*

5. *What are the four levels of church growth?*

    *1.*_____

    *2.*_____

    *3.*_____

    *4.*_____

6. *What happens at the Horse and Buggy Stage? Explain.*

7. *What happens at the "ER" Stage? Explain.*

Chapter Four

What Every Pastor Should Know

PLACE VISION STATEMENT ON EVERYTHING

Place your vision statement on everything. Everything! Place your vision statement on all the doors of the sanctuary, all the doors in the office, the church's letterhead, website, T-shirts, bulletins, banners, marquee, etc.... It is crucial for your people to know the vision. Habakkuk 2:2-3 says, "And the Lord answered me, and said, write the vision, and make it plain upon tables, that he may run that readeth it. For the vision is yet for an appointed time, but at the end it shall speak, and not lie: though it tarry, wait for it; because it will surely come, it will not tarry." The vision must be shared. Andy

Stanley, author of "Visioneering" said, "All God-ordained visions are shared visions. Nobody goes it alone. But God generally raises up a point person to paint a compelling verbal picture. A picture that captures the hearts and imaginations of those whom God is calling to embrace the task at hand."

Don't develop long vision statements. It may sound good, but if you can't put it to memory and place it in your heart, neither can the congregation. Your vision statement should be short, precise and to the point. Our vision statement at Voices of Faith is "To reach and disciple the unchurched with love and simplicity."

Use the space below to rewrite your vision statement. Remember, keep it short, precise and to the point:

_____

_____

_____

Once the vision is memorized, one can effectively witness for Jesus Christ. Learn to rid yourself of programs in the church that are not reflecting the vision. The quicker you close ineffective ministries in the church, the quicker you will see results.

Over 70 percent of the visitors attending our church are invited by our members. It is a good indicator that the vision is in full swing and effectively reaching the unchurched.

Can you think of seven areas in your church where your vision statement could be placed?

Write it down here:

1._____

2._____

3._____

4._____

5._____

6._____

7._____

PURPOSE DRIVEN ONLY!

Purpose driven only should be your church. What is your purpose? Pastors, when you know your purpose, when you know why God has called you to a ministry, you won't allow brush fires to side track you from reaching your destiny. Satan's job is to knock you off course. He does not want you to achieve greatness for God. Dr. I.V. Hilliard, author of "Mental Toughness For Success" said,

"There is a price for success which must be paid throughout the life of the pursuit in daily installments, but the most significant part of the price is not the daily installments, but the significant down payment which frightens most people away!"

Satan's job is to knock you off course.

The founder of McDonald's, the late Ray Kroc, several years ago spoke at a seminar and asked the question, what business is McDonald's in? One person raised his hand and said McDonald's is in the french fry business, he said no. Another said, McDonald's is in the hamburger business, he said no. Another said McDonald's is in the fast food business he said no. Ray Kroc said McDonald's is in the real estate business. Most McDonald's are on main highways and busy intersections. Ray Kroc understood his product must be exposed.

I encourage you to write your obituary. Write what you would want people to remember about you. Once you have completed your obituary quit working on assignments that have no or little significance in your life. When you know your purpose, you will focus only on things that matter most.

OLD LEADERS VERSUS NEW LEADERS

Your old leaders will seldom be your new leaders. God will bring people in your ministry to help you at different stages of ministry, but as you go to the next level, God will replace them with new leaders. I am always amazed at the awesomeness of God! Each time a leader leaves for whatever reason, God sends another who is better equipped for the journey. Each time God elevates your ministry, pruning and purging must take place. Don't get upset with leaders who threaten

> **Each time God elevates your ministry, pruning and purging must take place.**

to leave because they no longer are willing to submit to the new vision God has given you. Thank them for their service. That is God's way of pruning for a greater harvest. **Philippians 4:19** says, *"But my God shall supply all your need according to his riches in glory by Christ Jesus."*

SELECTING THE RIGHT BOARD MEMBERS

Selecting board members is one of the most crucial things you will ever have to do in ministry. Never select someone because of friendship and loyalty. There are three things you need to look for when selecting a board member. *First, they must be a Christian.* He or she has to be sold out for Christ. Their desire should be solely to please God. *Second, they must have a submissive spirit.* He or she cannot lead if they are not willing to follow. *Thirdly, they must be business minded.* Many pastors fail in this area. Pastors tend to select board members who have been with the ministry for a long period of time, but they have no vision. You cannot cast a vision with an individual who is use to handling small amounts of money. When God reveals a great vision that will involve millions of dollars, the board member who is not used to handling large amounts of money will vote against the vision. Small thinkers will cripple your vision.

Who are some people in your church that fit these three guidelines for selecting board members? List them here:

1._____

2._____

3._____

Deacon Greg Levett, one of my most faithful board members and servants for the Lord continues to push and encourage me to new heights. Recently, I was teaching a church growth seminar and to my amazement Greg Levett was in the audience attending the class. He owns two funeral homes in Atlanta. On this particular day, he was scheduled for several meetings and his company was extremely busy, but he canceled all appointments to support me during the seminar. He is saved, submissive, and an anointed businessman.

SUSTAINING GROWTH BEYOND YOUR STRUCTURE

You will never sustain growth beyond your structure. If you are structured for 100 people, on a good day, you may pack the house with 150, but you will return to 100 soon after. When your seating capacity is 100, you are not going to continue to increase your membership because folk will not want to come to an overcrowded church.

People like elbow room. Starting a new service will rectify overcrowding.

WHEN TO BEGIN TWO WORSHIP SERVICES?

You should begin a second service when you are out of parking or seats in worship service. Some have suggested when your parking lot is 80 percent full; a new worship service should be implemented. Timing is crucial. The time of year, can make or break your new service times. Spring and Fall are good times to start a new service because of Easter and the beginning of a new school year. Parents are settling back into a routine from vacations. Winter and Summer are bad times to start new worship services due to cold weather and families vacationing.

One of my members said, "Pastor, if we go to two worship services, the sanctuary will not be filled in either one." I told her, "I am not trying to fill every chair; I am trying to reach the needs of the people. The sanctuary will fill up if we reach their needs." There are people who will never attend your 8:00 a.m. service because they enjoy sleeping late. There are some who will never come to your 11:00 a.m. service because they are early risers. Having two services meets the needs of the people.

THE BENEFITS OF 2 SERVICES ARE GREAT

The benefits of two services are more people serving, more space, double attendance and double your offering. Our 8:00 a.m. worship service brings in more money than our 11:00 a.m. service even though more are in attendance at the 11:00 a.m. service.

MATCH PEOPLE'S GIFT TO A MINISTRY

Matching people's gift to ministry is one of the most difficult assignments. Too many people in the body of Christ are not operating in their gifts. Our deacons used to lead our devotion team during worship service, but the people were constantly arriving later and later for church. I polled the people to find out how to correct this dilemma. What I discovered was astonishing! Our devotion was killing the people. We had deacons praying, but were not gifted to pray. We had deacons singing, but were not anointed to sing. I immediately removed the deacons from conducting devotion. I replaced them with skilled people who are gifted to pray and anointed to sing. The results were instant success.

Dr. Samuel Chand, president of Beulah Heights Bible College in Atlanta, Georgia gave this analogy concerning matching people's gifts. There are three important steps to fulfill this task. **First**, *"Get the right people on the bus."* Make sure the people working in ministry are operating in their gift(s). I believe once an individual finds their calling, they will begin to maximize their fruits. **Second**, *"Get the wrong people off the bus."* Don't be afraid to remove people who are not operating in their gifts. The quicker this can be achieved the quicker success will take place in your ministry. **Finally**, *"Get the people on the bus in the right seat."* It is important when matching a person's gift to not just get them on the right bus, but to get them in their right seat. I believe many people are where God want them to be, however they are working on someone else's assignment. Dr. Chand who is also author of the book, "Futuring" said, "The right people in the right place create a winning team."

> ## Don't be afraid to remove people who are not operating in their gifts.

KEEPING FONT CONSISTENT

Keep your font consistent. This is one of the most common mistakes pastors and churches make when promoting their ministry. Always remain consistent when using fonts with your church's name on it. It creates identity and credibility. Your font will create an identity in itself. For example, Coca Cola uses the same font when advertising. Whether it's sponsoring a sporting event, commercial, or concert, Coca Cola's logo remains the same. Their logo has become the company's identity.

The font Voices of Faith uses to promote the ministry is "New Times Romans." We use it on the church's letterhead, website, television broadcast, marquee, billboards and many other media outlets. I've witnessed many churches changing their font on each new advertisement. It creates confusion and it suggests to potential members unstableness.

Make sure the font you select is easily readable. Remember you are not trying to impress people with beautiful letters, but you are trying to win them to Jesus Christ.

NEWSLETTER

A monthly church newsletter is a terrific way of marketing and informing members of future events. It can be used to promote birthdays and other special occasions. Make sure you select someone who has a passion for writing and a zest for finding unsung heroes in the church who can often go unnoticed working for God. Utilizing the newsletter to profile a new member is an excellent idea! It gives the new member an opportunity to express why they joined your church.

PICK YOUR BATTLES

One of the things pastors have not mastered is learning how to pick their battles. We spend too much time putting out brush fires. Brush fires are small fights and disagreements among the believers that can escalate into a wildfire. Some brush fires are not worth putting out. Every time you slow down to put out a brush fire, it delays you from reaching your destiny. You can't win all of them. Paul demonstrated this in Acts 16:16-34. Paul and Silas entered a city where a soothsayer was practicing witchcraft. She recognized Paul and Silas as men of God. She followed them for many days, but Paul ignored her. Finally, after many days of vexing Paul's spirit, he cast the demon out of her. Notice, Paul only responded after many days. She was not his assignment. Brush fires will slow you down. More people will leave your church from brush fires than for any other reason.

Never use God's pulpit to air out dirty laundry. God's pulpit is holy. God's pulpit is designed only to teach and preach His Word. I have witnessed too many preachers airing their problems and concerns about others in the pulpit.

NEVER MAKE SPIRITUAL DECISIONS ON FINANCE

Never make spiritual decisions based on your finances. God does not need money to bring about a miracle, He just needs our faith. Money follows faith. Dr. Samuel Chand suggests we ask ourselves four questions when making a spiritual decision for the church. **First,** *"Is this in line with our vision, mission or core values?"* I have discovered too many pastors are making decisions on major projects and programs that has nothing to do with their vision. Our vision is "to reach and disciple the unchurched with love and simplicity." One of the things we are doing to achieve our vision is broadcasting on television all over the United States. If you don't know where you are going, any road will get you there. **Second,** *"Do we have the heart for this?"* There will be people that will challenge your vision. They will criticize your decision-making, and they may even leave the church. Knowing what God called you to do is a must. Do you have the heart for the difficult task ahead? **Thirdly,** *"How will God be glorified?"* If I do this task, how will God get glory? If you are working on a project where God is not getting the glory, stop it immediately! Only what we do for Christ will last. **Finally,** *"How much will it cost?"* Money should be your last concern. If you can honestly

> **God does not need money to bring about a miracle, He just needs our faith.**

answer the first question, God will send you the money to complete the task at hand. Too many pastors weigh money as the primary concern before embarking on their vision. Remember money follows faith.

PRACTICAL AND RELEVANT MESSAGES

Many of us fail in this area of ministry. We are preaching messages that are not relating to the need of the people. Our messages should be practical and relevant to the daily life of the believer. Preaching about Daniel and the Lion's den and the three Hebrew boys, Shadrach, Meshach, and Abednego is meaningless if we cannot apply the story to the daily lives of the people. What does preaching about the valley of dry bones have to do with someone's spouse having an affair? What does preaching about Jesus walking on water have to do with me losing my job? We must be practical and relevant if we are going to reach God's hurting sheep.

Recently, I preached a three part series on harvest time. I dealt with their needs. Our country is in one of the worst recessions in history. Millions have lost jobs, life and health insurance, houses, cars, and personal items. My first message was "Plowing for a breakthrough." This message dealt with praise. Praise loosens up the dirt for your seed to germinate. The next sermon was "Cultivating your seed." This message spoke of turning over the soil and planting during a drought. A farmer doesn't plant at harvest time, he plants during the spring. It's in the winter months that he cultivates the dirt. The harvest comes during summer. The last message dealt with "The True Vine." This message portrays Jesus as the True Vine and us as the branches. As long as we are connected to Jesus, our lives will yield its maximum fruit. After the three week series, 150 people joined our ministry. I preached where they were hurting.

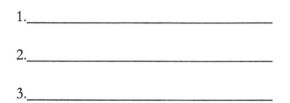

I preached where they were hurting.

What are some recent messages you preached that are relevant and practical? Write down three here:

1._____

2._____

3._____

THINK BIG

Growing a great church for God is a mindset. We often think at the level of our ministry. Eight years ago, we started Voices of Faith with only ten people, but I operated the church as if we were a mega ministry. Even though we were small in numbers, I never thought small. I was always about my Father's business of growing a great church for Him. I was not trying to please man, but my aim was to be in right relationship with God.

In the beginning of our ministry, we would only have 10 to 15 people show up each Sunday for worship. I would set up over 100 chairs even though a handful was attending. My brother, Aaron Hawkins, Jr., asked, "Why do you continue to set up all these chairs when you know only a handful of people will show?" My response, "The chairs I am setting up are not for the people who are coming today, but for the people I believe God will send tomorrow." I never thought with a small mindset. I always thought big!

> **We must be purpose driven to grow God's church.**

We must be purpose driven to grow God's church. We must have a strategy and goals to know whether you have achieved what you set out to accomplish. Dr. John Maxwell, author of "Developing The Leaders Around You" said, "People need clear objectives set before them if they are to achieve anything of value. Success never comes instantaneously. It comes from taking many small steps. A set of goals becomes a map a potential leader can follow in order to grow."

I remember when our total membership was 30 people. We had only a small amount of money in the bank. I remember driving down a busy highway noticing 20 acres of land. The Holy Spirit instructed me to make a u-turn and pray on the property. I believed God for the land. I contacted the owner of the property and he offered to sell the land for $300,000. The building we designed was going to cost us $450,000. I needed a loan for $750,000. I knew the bank would want a large down payment and at least three strong years of financial stability. We had recently lost over 200 members who had abandoned the ministry, yet 30 people, 15 were adults, I believed God for the land. I did not know how God was going to bless us, I just knew He would. My Minister of Finance, Mia Hawkins, who also is my sister-n-love, put together a business plan to take to the banks for a loan needed to purchase the property. After visiting several banks, one loan officer said, "I have never seen a more professional business plan for a church in 20 years of banking." An accountant, who audited our books said, "This is my very first church audit in 17 years where every "T" was crossed and every "I" was dotted right down to the penny." Needless to say, a few weeks later, a bank gave us the loan to purchase the property because we operated in a spirit of excellence. We never looked at ourselves as small. We always acted like more than conquerors. Proverbs 23:7 says, "For as he thinketh in his heart, so is he…" Thinking big pays great dividends!

Think of some things in your ministry that are impossible to accomplish alone. List seven things you desire that only God can provide. Pursue them as if your life depended on it. Write them here:

1._____

2._____

3._____

4._____

5._____

6._____

7._____

For Discussion

1. Why is it important to place your vision statements on everything in the church? Explain.

2. Is it important to be purpose driven in your church? Explain.

3. Do you feel selecting the right board members can be difficult?

4. When do you start a second worship service? Explain.

5. *What are the benefits of going to two worship services?*

6. *How important is matching people's gift to their ministry?*

7. *Why is it important to know when to pick your battles? Explain.*

Chapter Five

Creating a Healthy Church

ELIMINATE WASTEFULNESS DURING WORSHIP

C reating a healthy church should be your primary goal. Eliminating wastefulness during worship service is a great place to start. There is too much fat in the worship service that has nothing to do with God. The announcements are too long. It zaps the spirit in the church. Place the information on a bulletin and let them read it. Long drawn out announcements stop the anointing from flowing throughout the service.

Start worship service on time. If it is only one person in the sanctuary, start on time. Keep your word! The people must be trained to arrive on time to worship God. Don't keep the people more than two hours in service. Let them leave enjoying an experience, not tired from a fight.

Start worship service on time.

Keep tithes and offering to a minimum of ten minutes or less. We take up tithes and offering in less than five minutes. We achieve this by passing the offering basket around and not having the congregation march around. Take up one offering. Money is a sensitive subject in the church. There should be no down time during worship.

Serving communion should be done in less than 20 minutes. This can be accomplished by purchasing the "All in one cup." This cup contains both the bread and drink. The communion cup is also disposable.

What are some wasteful things in your church you can eliminate to grow a healthy church?
Write them down here:

1._____

2._____

3._____

4._____

5._____

ESCORTING NEW MEMBERS

The invitation is the most important time of the worship service. How you handle the invitation can determine the success of your ministry. Many traditional churches extend the invitation by asking people who do not have a relationship with God to give their lives to Jesus Christ by coming to the altar and publicly confessing Christ as Saviour. In front of the congregation, the pastor would ask each new member a series of questions concerning their salvation. He would ask questions such as: Are you saved? Have you given your life to Jesus Christ? Have you ever been baptized? Do you know the Lord as your personal Saviour? What's your name? Where are you from? Here's the dilemma with that process. The No. 1 fear in the world is public speaking. Many people are afraid to speak before large crowds therefore; it hinders the growth of your church when questions are asked in public before the congregation. We must remember that our goal is to reach the unchurched, not run them away. Rick Warren, author of "The Purpose Driven Church" said, "Since the church is a living organism, it is natural for it to grow if it is healthy. The church is a body, not a business. It is an organism, not an organization. It is alive. If a church is not growing, it is dying."

I remember as a teenager being frightened to death joining my church in Baton Rouge, Louisiana. After six months of procrastinating, I finally walked down the aisles with my knees shaking because I was afraid to speak before the church. I was terrified. I suggest you find a room in the church to minister to their needs.

At Voices of Faith, ministers, deacons and deaconess line up in the aisle ways and escort new members out of the sanctuary into a particular room in the church to min-ister to their needs without asking them embarrassing questions in pub-lic. There are trained ministers waiting in the rooms to find out their spiritu-al status with God. Now the new member can answer sensitive ques-tions freely without the church listen-ing to their every word. Make it easy for new members to make a decision.

> **One of the most powerful weapons we possess is giving someone a hug.**

Each new member gets a hug. One of the most power-ful weapons we possess is giving someone a hug. A hug breaks down stereotypes, barriers, and culture differences. When a new member decides Voices of Faith is where God has led them to join, ministers, deacons, and dea-conesses are waiting in the aisles to give each new mem-ber a hug. A hug is a powerful tool.

SETTING THE RIGHT ATMOSPHERE

Setting the right atmosphere for worship is critical for church growth. It starts with the parking ministry. It is very important to choose the right parking attendants for your church. Parking attendants are the first people visi-tors see upon arriving on your campus. They truly set the atmosphere for worship. Our Parking Ambassadors Ministry is truly remarkable! They change flat tires during worship service. They fix alternators and change batteries. They park ladies cars during the rain. They bring their bibles to minister to others and upon arriving on campus, each member and visitor gets a hug.

The greeters are also very critical to setting the atmosphere for worship. They greet you with a smile, they remember your name, and each member and visitor gets a hug. Make sure to select the right people in your greeters' ministry who can relate to people. It does not cease to amaze me how many churches have people working in the greeters' ministry with no people skills and with bad attitudes. It truly runs away the visitors.

The Gatekeepers Ministry (ushers) is another important ministry that sets the atmosphere for worship. Each member and visitor gets a hug. They escort you to your seat in a very **Try to be the friendliest church in town.** warm and friendly way. They are attentive and alert. The gatekeepers give each visitor a free audio tape of a previous week's message from the pastor. This has been truly successful. It has been one of the most powerful marketing tools at Voices of Faith. It doesn't cost much to buy a thirty-two cent audio tape that the church sells for five dollars. It gives them an opportunity to listen to the audio tape in the comfort of their own car.

Make the visitors remember their first visit for a life time. Try to be the friendliest church in town. You may not be the best preacher. You may not have the best choir in town. Your church may not be as breath taking as others, but you can pride yourself and church as being the friendliest in town. They may choose your church over many others. Make them glad they did. Thom Rainer, author of "Effective Evangelistic Churches" said, "More than any programmatic attempt to start community ministries in a church, the most effective ministries are those that develop from an atmosphere of love and concern."

Can you think of areas in your ministry that will set the atmosphere for worship?
Write them down here:

1._____

2._____

3._____

4._____

5._____

CALL ALL VISITORS YOURSELF

Pastors, this may be the granddaddy of them all! Calling all the visitors yourself each week is the most effective marketing tool. Don't delegate this task to anyone. Many have joined our ministry because I took the time to call.

Keep the conversation three minutes or less. Always acknowledge the man of the house. Often times a visitor is blown away to hear from the pastor. They may not be surprised by someone else in the church calling or writing a letter, but it blows their mind when it's the pastor. Don't ever feel calling visitors is beneath you. It is easy for me to make the call because I know my purpose. My purpose is to lead people to have a greater experience with Christ. It is truly to get folk saved.

Don't ever feel calling visitors is beneath you.

I get angry when very few people join our church. Often times I cannot sleep at night. I feel I have failed God. We average 30 new members a Sunday. A friend of mine, Shon Cooks, often calls after church asking how many joined today. I might say God blessed us with 35 new members. He would be so impressed, but he would detect sadness in my voice. He would say there are some churches that don't get 35 new members the entire year and you are upset because God only blessed you with 35. I let him know how grateful I am to God for sending 35 new members, but I knew in my heart there were many others that did not commit their lives to Christ. My purpose is to get folks saved. I'm not preaching for my health. I'm not preaching for myself. I'm preaching because God anointed me to get people saved. It bothers me when only a handful of people join church when I know the world is full of unchurched people. I go back praying asking God to give me a better understanding of how to reach His people. When I come to the podium to preach, I expect people to come down and give their lives to Jesus Christ. I expect it to happen. When I went to Jackson, Mississippi and preached at my good friend's church, Pastor Dwayne Pickett, 50 people gave their lives to Christ during the three day revival. I expected it. I am not being arrogant. I know God anointed me to lead His lost sheep to Christ.

SIX MARKS OF A GREAT LEADER

I had the pleasure of attending Xcel-Leadersip Conference 2002 led by Bill Purvis, pastor of Cascade Hills Baptist Church in Columbus, Georgia. Cascade Hills is one of the fastest-growing churches in the country. Here's a list of six things Bill Purvis mentioned a leader must possess to take his sheep to the next level and what makes up a leader.

1. Leaders see the **big** picture.
2. Leaders don't focus on **failure**; they focus on the goal.
3. Leaders take **risks**.
4. Leaders are willing to **change**.
5. Leaders pay the **price** others refuse to pay.
6. Real leaders are ordinary people with extraordinary **goals**.

Love those you lead.

- If you don't love them, you cannot lead them.

Empower your people.

- One of the mistakes pastors make is trying to do the ministries of the church instead of seeing that they get done.
- Never do ministry Alone. (Elijah, Elisha)
- Responsibility + Ownership.

Allow people to make mistakes

- Give them room to make mistakes. Failure can be our best teacher.

Develop potential leaders

- We teach what we know; we reproduce what we are.

Encourage their efforts

- Treat them like a "10" and they will begin to respond that way.
- Give praise for the willingness to serve.
- Brag on those who serve.

Reward your workers

- Be generous with tokens of appreciation.
- Reward staff with a day off.
- Take staff out to lunch.
- Bonus at Christmas.

For Discussion

1. Why is it important to eliminate wastefulness during worship service? Explain.

2. What is the number one fear in the world? Explain.

3. How can we set the right atmosphere in church?

4. Why are the greeters so critical in setting the atmosphere for worship?

5. Why is it important for the pastor to call the visitors? Explain.

6. What are the six marks of a great leader?

7. What does the acronym "L.E.A.D.E.R." means?

Chapter Six

How to Keep God's House Beautiful

WHAT YOU SEE IS WHAT YOU GET

K eeping the church attractive to visitors can play a major role in the growth of your church. Know that perception is reality. Whatever a visitor perceives about your ministry will become their reality. Your property should be designed to attract the visitor. Most visitors make up their mind about your ministry within the first five to seven minutes of arriving upon your campus.

> **Whatever a visitor perceives about your ministry will become their reality.**

It is extremely important to keep your parking area free from trash and debris. Keeping your property well manicured is a must to grow a great church for God.

Aaron Hawkins, Jr., my brother, taught a leadership class on "How to Keep God's House Beautiful" at Voices of Faith's "Faith to Faith" Pastor's and leadership Conference in November 2002. Here are some excerpts below from his class on Interior Motives and the Facilities Staff:

INTERIOR MOTIVES

"Keeping the inside well-groomed will be one of the first things a visitor will notice upon arriving in the sanctuary. It is important to place wastebaskets throughout the church to make it easier for church members to keep the church clean. You must be the example for how God's house is respected. Please know keeping God's house clean is a team effort. Encourage the ushers, greeters, and other church leaders and the pastor to make announcements regarding snacks and eating inside the church building.

Train ministries and auxiliaries to return all classrooms to the format in which they were found at the end of all meeting and training sessions. It is also important that your church look like a hospital. It should have directional signs on the grounds and in all areas of the building."

THE FACILITIES STAFF

"Keeping God's house clean is not an eight-hour a day job. It includes nights and weekends. When hiring for facility positions, it is very important to ensure that the individual(s) has a passion for keeping God's house clean. The facilities staff plays a vital role when it comes to keeping down church expenses. It is important that the facilities manager is a good steward over God's resources. When making purchasing decisions and ordering cleaning materials and supplies, make sure that you have done at least three price comparisons. Do your research; sometimes contracting services is more cost efficient than hiring someone on a full time basis."

For Discussion

1. Why is it so important to keep God's house beautiful? Explain.

2. Why do visitors make up their mind on whether or not they will return in the first five to seven minutes? Explain.

3. Why must each person take ownership in keeping God's house beautiful?

4. Is it important to train ministries and auxiliaries on how to keep the house of God beautiful?

5. Do you feel a well-groomed inside will attract visitors?

6. Explain why keeping God's house beautiful is not just an 8-hour day job.

7. Hiring for facility positions is crucial. Why?

Chapter Seven

Publicize Your Events Through the Media

WHAT IS NEWS?

One of the things that are hurting our churches today is a lack of knowledge on how to deal with the media. As your ministry gain exposure in your city, you will need to become more familiar with dealing with the media. Valerie Morgan, publisher of On Common Ground News, recently spoke at a leadership conference at our church giving tips on how to deal with the media. Here are some excerpts from her speech: "Ask anyone their definition of news and you're likely to get a variety of responses---from information about a police shooting that happened last night to a new commercial development under way.

81

But the media generally define news as controversy or change. Examine a newspaper or watch a newscast. Almost every story deals with change or controversy. To "make the news," you must be able to describe some change---a new product, a new direction or something that sets your ministry or company apart from the rest. This is the lynchpin in determining whether the media gives you news coverage."

TYPES OF MEDIA

Before we can pursue avenues to promote our churches, we must first understand the pros and cons of the types of media. So what are the advantages/disadvantages of print vs. broadcast? Printed news articles yield a clip---something that you can save, file, frame, or reference. Often times with printed articles, reporters can devote more time for a more in-depth news story. When you're interviewed, be sure and ask how the information will be used (as a news story, brief or mention), if that matters to you. But keep in mind the media's mission: to inform the public about change or controversy.

The media's mission: to inform the public about change or controversy.

With television, you obviously have greater exposure for a wider audience, but the time actually spent on you likely will be extremely limited. Interviews on air may last only a few seconds, with just a portion featuring you. With radio news stories, time also is extremely limited, unless you've been invited to appear on a talk show. If that is the case, you should request a format of the show and some idea of questions that you may be asked to avoid blundering.

For your consideration, however, the number of media outlets in this country is vast:

1,700 daily newspapers
Nearly a dozen national television networks
Four wire services, plus assorted syndicated services
8,000 cable systems
12,200 magazines

HOW IS NEWS GENERATED?

If you are going to place your ministry on the cutting edge to reach the unchurched, you must be resourceful and creative in generating publicity about your ministry. You must think the way a reporter will think. Reporters are looking to break a great story. In the future we plan to go to five grocery stores in the community **You must think the way a reporter will think.** to bag groceries for customers. We will not ask for anything (money, donations, etc...) in return. We just want to give back to the community. We will contact the local media because of the community oriented project.

Great results! Reporters and editors generate news through a number of resources including public records such as bankruptcy filings, court judgments, lawsuits, tax liens and building permits. They also glean leads and other information from press releases, e-mails, calendars, bulletin boards, tips from the public and community meetings.

Good journalists are extremely inquisitive and resourceful. They live and some even die---to fulfill an appetite to provide the public information.

As people, media tend to be:

1. Aggressive
2. Tough
3. Ethical
4. Fair

ENTICING THE EDITOR

How many of you have ever read in print the phrase "….. and a good time was had by all?" Don't ever send that outside of your church to the media! As a matter of fact, don't put that cliché in your church newsletters or bulletins. It is tired and does nothing at all to catch anyone's attention.

Editors and reporters receive dozens of faxes, phone calls and e-mails daily. In order to hook or entice the editor, you must capture their attention immediately with something that is going to make them hungry for a story.

If you can afford to hire a media specialist/communications director, it's a wise investment. If you cannot yet afford a staff position, you might consider hiring on an as-needed basis at an hourly rate or to work on special projects on a contract basis. Journalists are not only skilled at writing press releases. They are skilled at developing strong news angles that will get you the attention you are seeking when you need it. Also, a good journalist is skilled at handling adverse news. They will help you keep your foot out of your mouth.

Let's take a look at some church news events and how they might be handled: a Thanksgiving Day Dinner, a new church dedication, church growth. If you sent in basic information on these events, you would likely get just a mention in a big newspaper's calendar. However, you can tempt the media to do more, if your press release is well-written, timely, has the right angle, and you don't give yourself away that you're an amateur by using the phrase "and a good time was had by all." Here are some examples of how to hook an editor:

1. Voices of Faith Ministries is expecting lots of company for Thanksgiving Dinner: A group of 10 women are baking 300 turkeys, 50 trays of dressing and a field of collard greens.

2. The new sanctuary at Greater Beach Grove Ministries will be dedicated at 4:00 p.m. Sunday with a celebration service featuring guests from the community.

3. More than two months ago, Flatshoals Cathedral, a new congregation in Nashville, had an explosive first Sunday with 524 in attendance. Since then, the church staff has added a second service to accommodate another 650 worshippers who have been drawn to the church.

PREPARING YOUR PRESS RELEASE

Now that you've got the idea of how to entice the media, let's look at preparing your press release.

Are you trying to get someone to attend your conference, build up your membership, or attract new customers? Make sure you know what the mission is and how you will communicate that mission.

Sticking a sign out front and waiting for people to show up is not enough. You've got to get the word out and use as many vehicles as you can afford to communicate that mission.

Mrs. Morgan said, "Once the word is out, be prepared for response. This is especially important for churches. Too often, churches are accustomed to only announcing events to their congregations. They are not prepared to deal with the public at large. They have people who are not well-trained to answer the telephones or other inquiries and as a result, they ultimately hurt the church."

Valerie Morgan adds, "Recently, I contacted a well-established church and got a rude response when I attempted to find out if the church was planning to have a

Thanksgiving Day worship service. The pastor's executive assistant said that I should go to the Web site to find out anything I wanted to know about the church. So I thanked her and asked what time the normal worship services were and she gave me the Web site address. I asked why she couldn't give me the times and she mashed a button that put me into the church secretary's voice mail. I checked the Web address and all of the information was four months old!

The next day, I called back to speak with the pastor. The same woman told me that the pastor was booked with appointments until 2003. She said that she didn't have a calendar for 2003 and could not book me an appointment until her calendars came in! I was astonished that any pastor would have a person like this dealing with the public."

Here's my two cents worth to churches and businesses: Be careful of your instructions to people you leave in charge. The wrong person in a position like that can be a detriment to you and your organization.

Valerie Morgan adds, "I chose to leave that particular church out of the listing I was compiling. However, if I had been writing a negative news story, the pastor and the church would have been embarrassed. Reporters usually write that so-and-so could not be reached, which can be worse than responding."

PUTTING TOGETHER AN EFFECTIVE PRESS RELEASE

A press release can be extremely effective if the information is laid out in details. You can put together an effective press release by remembering the 5w's: Who, what, when, where, and why. To add color, you can include more background information. As an example, a cleanup is planned for a community on Nov. 12 at 10 a.m. Dumping is rampant and the neighbors are fighting back.

Know the audience that the news organization targets.

Good background information: One of the people leading the campaign is in a wheelchair and will roll along with the rest of the volunteers to do his part. Now, you've got good color for a story---not just an announcement.

Know the audience that the news organization targets. If you don't know this up front, you waste your time and the news organization's time. A community paper such as the Rockdale Citizen, for example, targets Rockdale County, Georgia. It is not likely to be interested in a Cobb County story, unless a Rockdale person, place or things are involved.

Establish a contact person at the news organization, and keep your source list updated. There is nothing more frustrating than sending your press release to the wrong person, both, for you and the wrong person. That release may or may not get passed on to the appropriate person.

Know what the deadlines are and meet them. Send information about upcoming events well ahead of time. This gives the news organization time to plan, set up interviews, pictures, etc.

It is important to develop a media contact list. Here is a list of things needed to keep records of your contacts:

1. Media name
2. Contact's Name/Title
3. Address
4. Telephone number
5. FAX
6. E-mail

GUIDELINES FOR GOOD PRESS RELATIONS

These three words will work wonders when dealing with the media: availability, reliability and credibility.

If reporters know you are available, they will call you before they call the competition. If you are reliable, you will have control over the story outcome because reporters are more likely to take you at your word. If you are credible, you will establish a long-term, mutually beneficial relationship with the media. Be up front. Tell the truth or nothing at all.

Never ignore the media's request for information or an

interview. Get back promptly. There is nothing like picking up the paper and reading that so-and-so did not return five phone calls. The public assumes you are guilty of something, and it's an embarrassment to you. No matter how you feel about the media, reporters won't go away. A reporter's job is not to please you. Their job is to gather information they believe is in the public interest. You can't bargain with or trade favors with a reporter. When dealing with negative news, never say "no comment" or "let's go off the record."

Never ignore the media's request for information or an interview.

The public generally accepts "no comment" as a self indictment---that you're hiding something. Don't give a reporter any information "off the record" that you wouldn't want to be made public. What you must always remember is that a reporter's job is to inform the public, to be a watchdog.

10 TIPS FOR GOOD INTERVIEWS

This list below was compiled from various sources to help educate you on how to interview with reporters:

1. Be up front and clear. Know how to define your messages concisely.
2. Be careful about giving your opinion.

3. Respond quickly to media requests. Deadlines are important.

4. Tell the truth or nothing at all.

5. Know your journalists.

6. Be aware of verbal and non-verbal communication.

Tell the truth or nothing at all.

7. Don't assume the media is abreast of the material sent prior to your interview.

8. Use anecdotes to establish credibility and increase interest.

9. Do not ignore the media's request for an interview or information.

10. Speak in sound bites. The simpler the message, the higher the retention rate.

Conclusion

We have become masters at building the church edifice, but we have not mastered how to draw people to them. There are many architecturally-designed churches that are absolutely breathtaking, yet many of the people in the church are lacking the oxygen to win souls for Christ. Darrell W. Robinson, author of "Total Church Life", said, "Wherever you may go, you will see buildings with signs in front. First Church, Community Church, and so forth. But the church is not buildings; it uses buildings. The church is not organization; it uses organization. It is not programs, although it uses programs. A local church is a body of baptized believers in Jesus Christ..."

Someone once said, "A business that fails to advertise is a business heading toward failure." Marketing is the new buzz word for the 21st century church. Exposure is the name of the game. We must expose Jesus Christ to the world. The church that refuses

> **We have become masters at building the church edifice, but we have not mastered how to draw people to them.**

to market Jesus Christ is a church that has plateaued and is dying.

We are God's salespeople and Jesus Christ is the product. We must convince people through our witnessing, testimonies, and creative marketing that once they have tried Jesus, their lives will never be the same.

I pray through the reading and implementation of these marketing concepts in this book, your ministry will explode! Exposing Christ to the world is the name of the game.

For Discussion

1. Name three media outlets in your area.

2. Name five creative things to entice the editor.

3. What are the 5w's to remember when putting together a press release?

4. List seven media contacts in your area.

5. What happens when you fail to advertise the church? Explain.

6. If we are God's salespeople, then who is Jesus Christ?

7. What is the buzz word for the 21st century church?

Bibliography

Barna, George
Grow Your Church From The Outside In
Ventura, California: Regal Books Publishers, 2002.

Chand, Samuel R.
Futuring
Grand Rapids, Michigan: Baker Books, 2002.

Hilliard, I.V.
Mental Toughness For Success
Houston, Texas: Light Publication, 1999.

Maxwell, John C.
Developing The Leaders Around You
Nashville, Tennessee: Thomas Nelson Publishers, 1995.

Maxwell, John C.
Failing Forward
Nashville, Tennessee: Thomas Nelson Publishers, 2000.

Morgan, Glenn and Valerie
On Common Ground News
Atlanta, Georgia: On Common Ground News Publishers, 2002

Purvis, Bill
XCEL-Leadership Conference
Columbus, Georgia: Cascade Hills Baptist Church, 2002.

Rainer, Thom
Effective Evangelistic Churches
Nashville, Tennessee: Broadman & Holman Publishers, 1996.

Robinson, Darrell W.
Total Church Life
Nashville, Tennessee: Broadman & Holman Publishers, 1997.

Sjogren, Steve
101 Ways To Reach Your Community
Colorado Springs, Colorado: NavPress, 2001.

Stanley, Andy
Visioneering Sisters
Oregon: Multnomah Publishers, 1999.

Towns, Elmer, Wagner, C. Peter, Rainer, Thom
The Everychurch Guide to Growth
Nashville, Tennessee: Broadman & Holman Publishers, 1998.

Warren, Rick
The Purpose Driven Church
Grand Rapids, Michigan: Zondervan Publishing House, 1995.